TRAVEL WITH THE GREAT EXPLORERS

Explore with

Marquette and Jolliet

Cynthia O'Brien

Crabtree Publishing Company

www.crabtreebooks.com

Crabtree Publishing Company
www.crabtreebooks.com

Author: Cynthia O'Brien

Managing Editor: Tim Cooke

Designer: Lynne Lennon

Picture Manager: Sophie Mortimer

Design Manager: Keith Davis

Editorial Director: Lindsey Lowe

Children's Publisher: Anne O'Daly

Crabtree Editorial Director: Kathy Middleton

Crabtree Editor: Petrice Custance

Proofreader: Wendy Scavuzzo

**Production coordinator
and prepress technician:** Tammy McGarr

Print coordinator: Katherine Berti

Written and produced for Crabtree Publishing Company
by Brown Bear Books

Library and Archives Canada Cataloguing in Publication

O'Brien, Cynthia (Cynthia J.), author
   Explore with Marquette and Jolliet / Cynthia O'Brien.

(Travel with the great explorers)
Includes index.
Issued in print and electronic formats.
ISBN 978-0-7787-2850-4 (hardback).--ISBN 978-0-7787-2854-2 (paperback).--ISBN 978-1-4271-7729-2 (html)

   1. Marquette, Jacques, 1637-1675--Juvenile literature. 2. Jolliet, Louis, 1645-1700--Juvenile literature. 3. Mississippi River Valley--Discovery and exploration--French--Juvenile literature. 4. Mississippi River Valley--History--To 1803--Juvenile literature. 5. Explorers--Mississippi River Valley--Biography--Juvenile literature. 6. Explorers--America--Biography--Juvenile literature. 7. Explorers--France--Biography--Juvenile literature. I. Title. II. Series: Travel with the great explorers

F352.O27 2016   j910.92'2   C2016-903347-3
                                           C2016-903348-1

Library of Congress Cataloging-in-Publication Data

Names: O'Brien, Cynthia (Cynthia J.), author.
Title: Explore with Marquette and Jolliet / Cynthia O'Brien.
Description: New York, New York : Crabtree Publishing Company, [2016] | Series: Travel with the great explorers | Includes index.
Identifiers: LCCN 2016023868 (print) | LCCN 2016024184 (ebook) | ISBN 9780778728504 (reinforced library binding) | ISBN 9780778728542 (pbk.) | ISBN 9781427177292 (electronic HTML)
Subjects: LCSH: Marquette, Jacques, 1637-1675--Juvenile literature. | Joliet, Louis, 1645-1700--Juvenile literature. | Mississippi River Valley--Discovery and exploration--French--Juvenile literature. | Mississippi River Valley--History--To 1803--Juvenile literature. | Explorers--Mississippi River Valley--Biography--Juvenile literature. | Explorers--America--Biography--Juvenile literature. | Explorers--France--Biography--Juvenile literature.
Classification: LCC F352 .O27 2016 (print) | LCC F352 (ebook) | DDC 910.092/2 [B] --dc23
LC record available at https://lccn.loc.gov/2016023868

Crabtree Publishing Company

www.crabtreebooks.com   1-800-387-7650

Printed in Canada/072016/EF20160630

**Published in Canada
Crabtree Publishing**
616 Welland Ave.
St. Catharines, ON
L2M 5V6

**Published in the United States
Crabtree Publishing**
PMB 59051
350 Fifth Avenue, 59th Floor
New York, New York 10118

**Published in the United Kingdom
Crabtree Publishing**
Maritime House
Basin Road North, Hove
BN41 1WR

**Published in Australia
Crabtree Publishing**
3 Charles Street
Coburg North
VIC, 3058

CONTENTS

Meet the Boss

In 1673, Father Jacques Marquette and Louis Jolliet teamed up to explore the mighty Mississippi River. They came from different backgrounds and had separate ambitions—but together they made history.

Did you know ?

The Jesuits were founded in 1540 by Ignatius of Loyola, who wanted to spread the Catholic faith. He thought priests should have military-type discipline. Loyola called his followers "Soldiers of Christ."

MISSION TO THE NEW WORLD

+ Called to the priesthood

+ Moves to New World

Jacques Marquette (right) was born in 1637. He was the sixth child born into a wealthy French family. At age 17, Marquette began studying to become a **Jesuit** priest. He wanted to be a **missionary** and spread the Catholic faith in the New World, which is now known as North America. "This has been my thought since my earliest childhood," he wrote. In 1666, he arrived in New France, the French colony in what is now Canada.

LEARNING THE LINGO

★ Language skills...

★ ... help to spread the message

After he arrived in New France in 1666, Marquette spent two years studying the **dialects** of local Native languages, such as Algonquian and Iroquoian. This proved useful later, when he met and camped with people on his travels. He was able to communicate with them and learn about their cultures. The Jesuits sent Marquette to the city of Sault Sainte Marie in the Great Lakes region. He soon left to set up his own **mission**, St. Ignace, in what is now Michigan.

A CANADIAN EXPLORER

☛ **Young man trains for priesthood**

☛ **Then chooses new path**

Louis Jolliet was born in 1645 near Quebec, a settlement in New France. His father, Jean, repaired wagons. As a boy, Jolliet attended a Jesuit college. At age 17, he began studying for the priesthood but he soon changed his mind. Instead, he left for France to study **cartography** for a year. When he returned to New France, he decided to look for a life of adventure.

IT RUNS IN THE FAMILY

+ Life in the wilderness

Jolliet's older brother, Adrien, was a fur trapper. When Jolliet returned from France, he decided to join Adrien and become a **coureur de bois**. Jolliet learned to speak the languages of the Algonquian people and traveled across the **wilderness** to Sault Sainte Marie. There, in June 1671, Jolliet was one of the men who signed a declaration claiming a vast area of land for King Louis XIV of France.

LET'S GO!

★ **Explorers team up**

Native peoples around Lake Michigan talked about the "Misi-ziibi," which means "big river" in Ojibwe. Father Claude-Jean Allouez, a Jesuit missionary, heard these stories in the early 1670s. The French wanted to explore more of North America. It is not clear when Jolliet and Marquette first met. They may have known each other in Quebec or Sault Sainte Marie. In 1673, the two men decided to find and explore the "Big River."

Where Are We Heading?

From the Great Lakes region, Jolliet and Marquette headed southwest. They mapped one of the greatest rivers in North America—the mighty Mississippi.

Big River

The Mississippi is 2,320 miles (3,730 km) long. It flows from northern Minnesota to the Gulf of Mexico. The river's many tributaries flow through 31 US states and two Canadian provinces.

STINKING BAY

☞ New land...

☞ ... made out of mud

From the mission at St. Ignace, Marquette and Jolliet traveled to Green Bay on Lake Michigan. The French called the basin "Baye des Puans," or "Stinking Bay," but no one knows why. Marquette claimed that the water was full of "mire and mud." He and Jolliet passed through the area in the spring, so the conditions may have been damp and muddy. From Green Bay, the explorers sailed down the Fox River.

TRAVEL UPDATE

Take a tip from the locals

★ If you're traveling in unknown lands, get some local help. Marquette and Jolliet were guided by two members of the Mascouten tribe, who lived in what is now Wisconsin. The guides helped the Europeans sail down a wide, sandy river the Native peoples called the Meskousing. Today it is called the Wisconsin River. It flows through a varied landscape of hills, forests, and prairies.

❝ Its current, which flows southward, is slow and gentle. To the right is a large chain of very high mountains, and to the left are beautiful lands." *Jacques Marquette describes reaching the Mississippi River.*

THE BIG RIVER

+ Reaching the big river

On June 10, 1673, Jolliet and Marquette arrived at the point where the Wisconsin River meets the Mississippi (above). This is now Prairie du Chien, Wisconsin. As the expedition entered the Mississippi, Marquette wrote that he was full of "a joy I cannot express." The explorers had reached their first goal.

FIRST ONE TO THE EAST

★ **Rumored route to Asia**

★ **But where is it?**

From the 1500s, the Europeans had been searching for the Northwest Passage. This was a fabled water route through North America to the Pacific Ocean and Asia—and to its riches, such as spices. Jolliet hoped that the "big river" might be this route. However, Jolliet soon realized the river flowed south, leading to the Gulf of Mexico, not the Pacific Ocean.

LET'S TAKE A SHORTCUT

★ **A new route home**

★ **Crossing the prairies**

When the expedition headed back up the Mississippi, the explorers decided to travel along the Illinois River as a quicker way back to Green Bay. This allowed them to map another river and meet new people. Marquette also made notes and sketches of the amazing variety of wildlife on the prairies.

MARQUETTE AND JOLLIET'S VOYAGE ON THE MISSISSIPPI

Louis Jolliet and Jacques Marquette traveled nearly 1,100 miles (1,770 km) down the Mississippi, from the mouth of the Wisconsin River to the mouth of the Arkansas—and that was just one part of their journey.

Sault Sainte Marie

St. Ignace

Wisconsin River →

Green Bay

GREAT LAKES

NORTH AMERICA

Green Bay
The expedition reached Green Bay, where they met the Mascouten, Miami, and Kisabou peoples. Guides took them to what the Native peoples called the Meskousing, now known as the Wisconsin River.

Illinois Village

Mississippi River

Mississippi
The explorers sailed from the Wisconsin into the Mississippi River on June 17, 1673. Marquette wrote that he felt an "overwhelming joy."

Arkansas River

SPANISH TERRITORY

Illinois Village
After about a week on the Mississippi, the expedition reached a village of the Illinois people that Marquette noted had at least 300 dwellings. The explorers were welcomed with a feast and shown around the village, where they were given gifts.

Arkansas

Arkansas
While visiting the Arkansas, or Quapaw, the explorers heard that there were Europeans farther south on the Mississippi. They realized they must be Spaniards. Not wishing to come into conflict with France's enemies, they turned for home on July 17, 1673.

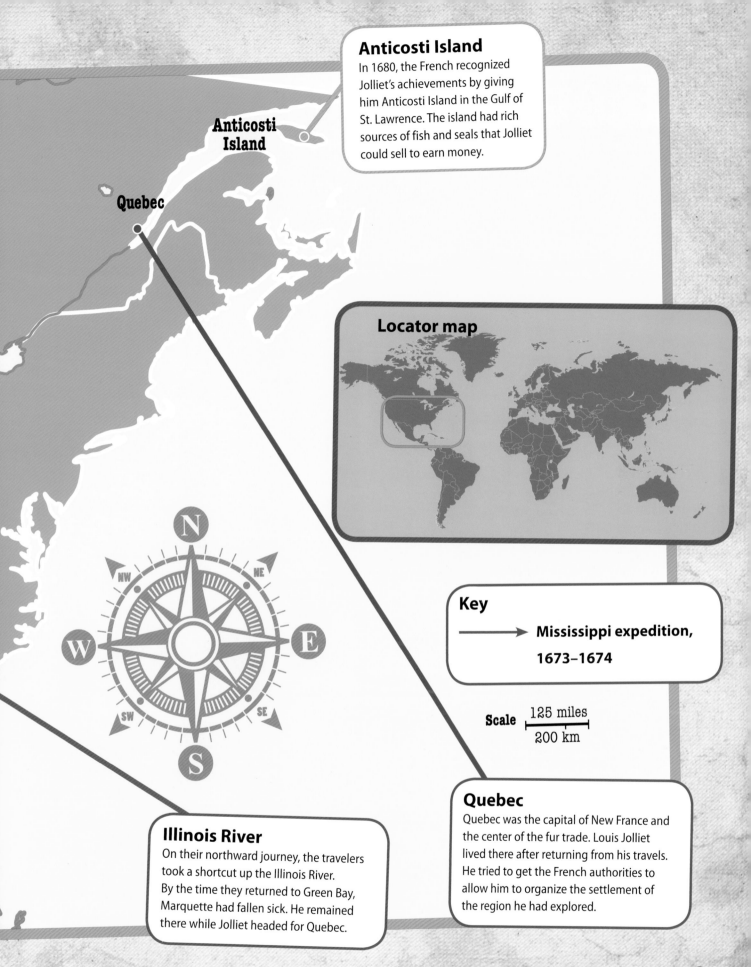

Anticosti Island
In 1680, the French recognized Jolliet's achievements by giving him Anticosti Island in the Gulf of St. Lawrence. The island had rich sources of fish and seals that Jolliet could sell to earn money.

Anticosti Island

Quebec

Locator map

Key

⟶ **Mississippi expedition, 1673–1674**

Scale 125 miles / 200 km

Illinois River
On their northward journey, the travelers took a shortcut up the Illinois River. By the time they returned to Green Bay, Marquette had fallen sick. He remained there while Jolliet headed for Quebec.

Quebec
Quebec was the capital of New France and the center of the fur trade. Louis Jolliet lived there after returning from his travels. He tried to get the French authorities to allow him to organize the settlement of the region he had explored.

Meet the Crew

From cash-hungry governors to a loyal wife, many people helped Jolliet and Marquette along the way. They provided money, inspiration, and other necessities for the explorers.

Fur Trade

In the 1600s, the fur trade was very important. There was a huge demand in Europe for North American furs. Beaver was particularly popular. It could be polished to a shiny finish and used to make hats.

A GUIDING HAND

+ Pioneer missionary

+ Reports stories about "big river"

Father Claude-Jean Allouez was a Jesuit who established missions in what is now Michigan, Wisconsin, and Minnesota. He lived among the native people for more than 20 years, learning their languages and customs and teaching them about Christian beliefs (right). In 1669, the young Marquette arrived at the mission at La Pointe du Saint Esprit to take over from Allouez. Father Allouez told Marquette about a mighty river to the south.

ALONG FOR THE RIDE

★ Fur trappers lend a hand

★ Used to frontier conditions

The government in New France would not fund the expedition, so Jolliet raised money by signing a contract with seven other men. He agreed to share any **profits** with them, although he would take half. Five of the men were experienced trappers. They agreed to join the expedition.

SHOW ME THE MONEY

☛ **Investors fund Jolliet's plans**

Jolliet was a businessperson as well as a trapper. In addition to the five fur trappers, he needed other **investors** for his expedition. He turned to his longtime business partner François de Chavigny, and his younger brother Zacharie Jolliet. The two investors hoped to profit from the expedition, but did not go along. Chavigny stayed in New France while Zacharie looked after the Jolliet family fur-trading business at Sault Sainte Marie.

WEDDING BELLS FOR JOLLIET

★ **Explorer marries**

In 1675, Jolliet married Claire-Françoise Bissot, the daughter of a wealthy Quebec fur trader. The couple had several children. They also inherited land in Labrador. Later, Jolliet was given the right to govern the island of Anticosti as a reward for his explorations. In 1690, while Jolliet was away, the English captured the island, briefly taking Claire-Françoise and her mother prisoner.

My Explorer Journal

★ **Imagine that Jolliet has asked you to invest in his expedition. What sort of arguments would persuade you to risk your money in a scheme that might not succeed?**

ON GOVERNOR'S ORDERS

+ **Frontenac sends Jolliet west**

In 1672, Louis de Buade de Frontenac (left) became governor of New France. The previous governor had already asked Jolliet to find the Mississippi, and Frontenac backed the decision. He hoped Jolliet's explorations would expand France's territory in the New World. He also hoped Jolliet might find a route to China and the riches of the East.

Check Out the Ride

In the 1600s, explorers and settlers in North America learned how to travel like the locals—by canoe. They paddled for miles across lakes, down wide rivers, and along narrow streams.

Did you know?

Algonquin canoes were 40 feet (12 m) long and weighed less than 300 pounds (136 kg), but they were very strong. Each canoe could carry about 12 men and their supplies.

THE ONLY WAY TO TRAVEL

+ Locals provide the transport

Jolliet and Marquette learned to make canoes by copying Native peoples. Native builders used thin sheets of bark from a birch tree to cover a frame made from cedar wood, which is light and resists decay. They sewed the bark to the frame using thread made from spruce roots. Finally, the builders used spruce gum to **caulk** the seams and make the canoes watertight.

DANGER AHEAD!

☛ Keep clear of trouble

☛ Get out and walk

River **rapids** could be dangerous and unpredictable, so the explorers avoided them by carrying their boats along the river to safer water beyond the rapids. Birch bark canoes were light enough to carry, making the **portage** easier. They also portaged between different rivers, especially where they were close to the river sources.

Weather Forecast

COVER UP IN THE SUN!

As the expedition traveled south down the Mississippi River, the climate grew hotter. Jolliet and Marquette used canvas sails to cover their canoes. These protected the travelers from the hot sun—and kept off the swarms of mosquitoes.

My Explorer Journal

★ Imagine you were one of the explorers paddling a canoe for hours every day. How do you think you would pass the time to prevent boredom?

TRAVEL UPDATE

Going against the current!

★ Remember that traveling upstream is harder work than floating with the current—make sure you save some energy for the journey home! Marquette and Jolliet found it difficult to travel north on the Mississippi and Illinois rivers. The explorers and their companions needed all their strength to paddle against the strong current.

Safety First

The explorers' birch bark canoes provided safe sleeping quarters. If the Frenchmen were worried that Native peoples on the shore might be hostile, they anchored out on the river for the night.

EXPLORE WITH MARQUETTE AND JOLLIET **13**

Solve It With Science

The explorers' survival kit ranged from natural remedies they had learned from Native peoples to the latest advances in **navigation** equipment.

Mapping

When Jolliet mapped the Mississippi, he made careful note of the rivers that joined it. He hoped that one of the rivers that flowed from the west might offer a water route to Asia—the fabled Northwest Passage.

MAPPING THE MISSISSIPPI

+ Jolliet shows off his talents

+ Latest in navigation technology

As a young man, Louis Jolliet spent a year in France studying valuable skills. He became an expert at cartography and **hydrography**, or the measurement of bodies of water. Back in New France, this helped to convince Governor Frontenac that Jolliet would be a good leader for the expedition. To navigate and create his maps, Jolliet used a **compass**, for direction. He also carried an astrolabe (right). This instrument measures the height and position of the stars, planets, Sun, and Moon, and it helped navigators figure out their position and time of day.

HEALING HERBS

★ Watch out for snakebites

★ Natural remedy available

Native peoples knew many ways to use plants as medicines. Father Allouez told Marquette about a plant root that could help with the effects of snakebite. Marquette wrote that the root was "**pungent**" and should be chewed, then spread over the bite. Since snakes were common in the area, Marquette collected many plants to take on his journey.

> "It is very pungent, and tastes like powder when crushed with the teeth; it must be chewed and placed upon the bite inflicted by the snake." *Marquette describes a healing plant.*

My Explorer Journal

★ Imagine you are in charge of packing for the Mississippi expedition. What tools and equipment should you take? Make a list of everything you think you would need.

BOOM!

☛ Gunpowder used by Europeans...

☛ ...and by Native peoples

Before Europeans arrived in North America, most Native peoples used spears or bows and arrows for hunting and warfare. Europeans brought guns and wore pouches containing bullets and powder horns for gunpowder (below). Marquette and Jolliet were surprised when they met the Chickasaw peoples, near modern-day Memphis. The Chickasaw had traded with the English in the east for goods, so they already had supplies of guns and gunpowder.

WHICH WAY TO THE MISSISSIPPI?

★ Gathering information

Before setting out from St. Ignace, Jolliet collected all the information he could find about the area he would be exploring. He spoke to Native peoples and used their stories to make a rough map of the journey. He used this for navigation, and updated it as the expedition traveled south.

Hanging at Home

Explorers in the New World were used to hardship. They had to hunt for their food—although sometimes they met friendly peoples who welcomed them with meals.

Did you know?

Jolliet was a trained musician. He played the organ and the harpsichord. On the trip, he was very interested in the Native music he heard. He wrote down the music of an Illinois song.

IT'S ALL ABOUT THE GAME

☛ Food for everyone

☛ Hunters bag provisions

Having enough food was vital on a long expedition. Jolliet made sure there was plenty of corn and dried meat on the canoes. However, all of the men were experienced at surviving in the wilderness. They were excellent hunters and could track game, such as deer. This gave them a good supply of fresh meat. They also found plenty of fruit, such as mulberries, and nuts such as pecans. The food kept them healthy and strong.

WOOF! WOOF!

★ Illinois offer an unusual treat

★ Travelers politely refuse

The Illinois greeted the explorers warmly. They served a feast including **sagamity** (left), a porridge made from corn. Fish and buffalo were also on the menu. Only one dish was not welcome: "a large dog that had just been killed." Dog meat was a treat in the Illinois culture, but Marquette explained that the French did not eat dogs.

TRAVEL UPDATE

Use your hands

★ When meeting new Native peoples, you might have to try new ways to communicate. Although both Jolliet and Marquette spoke several Algonquian and Huron languages, this was only useful on the northern part of their journey. As they moved south, they met peoples such as the Michigamea who spoke different languages. The Europeans used their guides as translators. They were also able to communicate with Native peoples by using their hands and creating a kind of sign language.

PADDLE YOUR OWN CANOE

★ **Team effort**

★ **Jobs for everyone**

The men on the expedition all had to help one another succeed. Jolliet was the group's leader and mapmaker, and an expert trapper. Marquette provided **spiritual** guidance, but also spoke many languages and recorded the expedition in his journal. The other men took turns looking out for hazards, as well as paddling, cooking, hunting, and fishing. Meanwhile, the Native guides had valuable knowledge about the land and acted as **interpreters**.

Meeting and Greeting

Many Native peoples lived in North America in the 1600s. They welcomed the explorers and gave them food, a place to sleep, and some lifesaving advice.

Did you know?

The Illinois gave the explorers a calumet, or tobacco pipe. It had white feathers on it as a symbol of peace. The explorers used it to show strangers that they meant no harm. The Illinois chief also sent his young son to act as a guide for the explorers.

HANGING WITH THE MASCOUTEN

★ Lowdown from the locals

★ Mascouten know the way

After leaving the Fox River, the explorers came across a Mascouten village where they were welcomed. Miami and Kickapoo people also lived in the area. The Mascouten told the Frenchmen how to reach another river, the Wisconsin, which they said led to the Mississippi. Two Miami guides took the explorers to the Wisconsin.

WARNING! DANGER!

☛ Menominee tell strange tales

☛ Explorers not put off

Marquette and Jolliet met the Menominee people at the St. Francis Xavier mission on the Fox River. Their name means "white rice people" in Ojibwe. The Menominee tried to stop the explorers from heading to the Mississippi. They said the "big river" was full of monsters and that the people to the south were hostile. The Menominee were traders. They may have told such stories to protect their trading relationships with other Native peoples and keep the French away.

HEY, I RECOGNIZE THOSE CLOTHES!

+ Marquette wears black clothes

+ Makes favorable impression

About a month into their journey, Jolliet and Marquette met the Illinois. From their canoes, the explorers noticed some tracks on the shore, which they followed to a village. The villagers were reassured to see Marquette's black Jesuit robes. Other Jesuits had visited the village before, so they knew that Marquette was not a threat. The Illinois offered the explorers pipes to smoke. Later, they had a great feast and made a speech welcoming their guests.

Driven Out

In the 1700s, the Fox Wars led by the French drove the Mascouten and their allies west. The Mascouten merged with the Kickapoo and no longer existed as an independent nation.

Weather Forecast

THE WAY OF THE ILLINOIS

The Illinois, or Illini, moved around the Mississippi Valley depending on the season. In summer they lived in large villages (right) where they grew crops such as corn. Marquette counted 300 cabins when he visited the Illinois. In winter, the Illinois moved to smaller villages of oval-shaped **wigwams**. Illinois women farmed, cooked, and built shelters, while the men hunted, fished, or defended the village.

More Encounters

As their journey down the Mississippi continued, Marquette and Jolliet met more Native peoples—and made sure they avoided other Europeans to the south.

Chickasaw

Marquette thought the Chickasaw looked like the Huron, a Native people he met in New France. However, the Chickasaw did not speak a Huron language. The explorers communicated with them by hand signals.

CONVERSATION WITH THE CHICKASAW

★ A quick bite...

★ ... and the explorers are gone

The Chickasaw lived east of the Mississippi. They were skilled warriors who fought with their neighbors, the Choctaws, and captured them as slaves. They traded the slaves with the English in neighboring Carolina in return for guns and other goods. The explorers shared meat and wild plums with the Chickasaw, who gave them good news— they were no more than ten days from the sea.

PROCEED WITH CAUTION

☛ Scary encounter on the river

☛ Calumet proves valuable

The Frenchmen spent an uneasy time with the Michigamea. At first meeting, the Michigamea appeared hostile. They approached the visitors' canoes, waving their weapons. Marquette held up the calumet the Illinois had given him (right). The Michigamea saw this as a gesture of peace and invited the explorers to their village for food.

DON'T GO ANY FARTHER!

+ Tribe warns of trouble ahead

+ Quapaw hostile toward Chickasaw

The Michigamea told the explorers they would get more information from the Arkansas people to the south. This was their name for the Quapaw, who lived west of the Mississippi in modern-day Arkansas (right). As Marquette and Jolliet neared the village, the Quapaw traveled out to meet them, holding a calumet. The Quapaw were eager to make an alliance with the French. They explained that their enemies, the Chickasaw, would not allow them to trade with the Spanish or the English, and kept the trade for themselves. The Quapaw warned the explorers that there were dangerous tribes and Europeans to the south.

My Explorer Journal

★ Imagine you are a member of the expedition. Write a letter to the governor of New France to tell him about some of the people you have met. Include a drawing.

THE SPANISH PROBLEM

☛ Enemy to the south

☛ Risk of conflict

When the Quapaw told the explorers about Europeans to the south, the Frenchmen knew they meant the Spanish. A Spanish explorer named Hernando de Soto had crossed the Mississippi a century earlier (left) and met the Chickasaw. By 1673, the Spanish had claimed territory in Florida, Texas, and parts of the Southwest. The Frenchmen feared being captured by the Spaniards if they went farther south. They decided to go back to New France with the information they had gathered.

I Love Nature

The explorers gazed across wide prairies and traveled through lush river valleys. They were amazed at the towering trees and the stunningly colorful birds.

Watch Out!

Among the other new animals the explorers saw were buffalo, or bison. The Frenchmen were amazed by the vast herds of buffalo roaming the prairies. They described how a buffalo could toss a person on its horns!

BRILLIANT BIRDS

+ Colorful birds everywhere...

+ ... but now gone

As they paddled down the Mississippi, the explorers saw huge, noisy flocks of bright green birds with yellow and red heads. They were Carolina parakeets, and they lived in forests along the rivers from south Wisconsin to the Gulf of Mexico. The bird was the only parrot native to North America. Over time, settlers cleared the land and destroyed the parakeet's forest habitat. Hunters killed them for their feathers and farmers shot them as pests. The last wild parakeet was shot in 1904. In 1939, the Carolina parakeet was declared **extinct**.

I'LL HAVE SOME MORE

★ **Marquette tries a native dish**

★ **Wild oats resemble rice**

Wild rice grew in shallow rivers around the Menominee settlements in Wisconsin. Marquette called the plant and the people "folle avoine," or wild oats. The Menominee harvested the grain by shaking the long stalks into their canoes. They dried the grain over log fires or by laying it out in the sun. Women pounded the dry rice into flour or boiled it. Marquette wrote that the "wild oats have almost as delicate a taste as rice."

NORTH AMERICAN GIANTS

☞ Tree-lined banks...

☞ ... covered in cotton

Marquette and Jolliet admired the tall gum, elm, and cottonwood trees they saw along the river. The cottonwood (right) is a large tree that grows up to 80 feet (24 m) tall. The trees produce seeds covered in cottony hair, which helps the wind to carry and deposit the seeds across large areas. Plains peoples used the cottonwood bark and leaves in medicines.

TRAVEL UPDATE

Painted monsters

★ On the Mississippi, the explorers saw two monsters painted on rocks high above the river. Marquette said the monsters had "horns on their heads," "red eyes," and bodies "covered in scales." The painting may have shown an evil, dragonlike creature called the "Piasa." The Illinois people believed it had preyed on humans until brave warriors killed it.

Did you know?

The rock paintings of monsters above the Mississippi River no longer exist. One reason is that Native peoples fired their guns at the rock face each time they passed by on the river.

FISH ATTACK

★ Fish with whiskers

★ Giant catfish threaten canoes

Many catfish (left) lived in the Mississippi River, where Native peoples caught them for food. Marquette called them "monstrous fish" with "the head of a tiger...with whiskers." The fish were so large that they crashed into the explorers' canoe and almost sank it. Catfish get their name from their large feelers, which look like cat whiskers.

Fortune Hunting

Louis Jolliet wanted to expand his fur business, and to help the French increase their influence in North America. Jacques Marquette, meanwhile, saw the trip as a chance to spread his Christian message.

Weather Forecast

AN IDEAL LOCATION!

The prairies of Illinois (right) enjoyed a mild climate, with warm summers and cool winters. Jolliet thought they would make good farmland. There were few trees, making it easier to plant crops. Back in New France, Jolliet asked if he could **colonize** Illinois. The French refused. They said they wanted to settle more people in New France before expanding into other lands.

MISSED OPPORTUNITY

+ Jolliet focuses on exploration

One reason Jolliet made his journey to the Mississippi was to expand the fur trade. The French already controlled the fur trade in New France, from Quebec to the Great Lakes. The Jolliet family were successful fur traders. Instead of paying for the expedition, Governor Frontenac gave Jolliet and his partners the right to trade in any new territories they visited. Jolliet was too busy exploring on the journey to trap any furs, but other French trappers did move into the area later (right).

THE BLACK ROBES

- Seeking spiritual rewards
- On a mission to save souls

Native peoples called the Jesuits "Black Robes" because of their clothes. The Black Robes were not interested in making money. They wanted to spread Christianity in the New World and **converts** people. They had few successes. However, Marquette did find willing listeners among the Kaskaskia people along the upper Illinois River (right). He returned for a short time in 1675 to establish the Immaculate Conception mission.

CHECKING OUT THE COMPETITION

★ Jolliet's fact-finding journey

Jolliet returned to work in the fur trade after his Mississippi expedition. The French and the English were fierce competitors. In 1679, Jolliet traveled north to Hudson's Bay (below left) to investigate the English fur trade there. He was impressed by how many furs they gathered. He recommended that the French drive the English from the area to protect the rich source of furs there. The English asked Jolliet to work for them, but he refused.

TRAVEL UPDATE

Highway to the gulf

★ Jolliet and Marquette did not find the Northwest Passage—a route to the Pacific—but Jolliet thought a **canal** from Lake Michigan to the Illinois River could create a water route from the St. Lawrence through the Great Lakes to the Mississippi and the Gulf of Mexico. However, the French were only interested in a route to the Pacific. They refused to consider building a canal.

This Isn't What It Said in the Brochure!

There were times, both on their journey and afterward, when Marquette and Jolliet found themselves facing unexpected problems and disappointments.

Did you know?

In 1678, the French king sent Sieur de La Salle to explore and colonize lands west and south of New France. Just a few years earlier, France had refused Jolliet's request to start a settlement in Illinois.

WE'RE SURROUNDED

- A Disappointing Arrival

- Violent Resistance

On the Mississippi, after leaving the Illinois people, the explorers heard cries from the shore. Suddenly, warriors appeared "armed with bows, arrows, hatchets, clubs, and shields." They set out toward the explorers' canoes. They ignored Marquette as he raised the calumet in greeting. Only the actions of two Native leaders stopped the attack. The Europeans stayed one night in the Native village and left the next morning.

OVERTURNED!

★ Journals lost in rapids

★ Key records destroyed

After the expedition, Jolliet left Marquette at Green Bay and set off back to Quebec. Rather than go on a long portage, he decided to canoe through the Lachine Rapids, near Montreal. Jolliet's canoe **capsized**. Two companions and the young Illinois guide drowned. Jolliet clung to rocks for four hours until rescuers arrived. All his notes and maps sank into the St. Lawrence.

I DON'T BELIEVE YOU!

+ Explorer's stories fail to impress

Jolliet returned to Quebec (below) to a disappointing reception. He had expected some recognition and financial reward for his expedition. He also hoped to explore the rivers west of the Mississippi in the hopes of finding a route to the Pacific. The French authorities doubted his stories, however, because Jolliet lost his reports and maps in the canoe accident. There was no proof to back up his claims. Then the explorer received even more devastating news. The copies of his notes he had made and left at Sault Sainte Marie were destroyed in a fire. Jolliet had no choice but to rewrite his notes and draw a new map from memory.

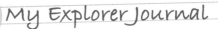

My Explorer Journal

★ Imagine you were living in Quebec when Jolliet returned. When you heard his stories of the "Big River" do you think you would believe them or not? Give your reasons.

Fire!

Jolliet lost the copies he made of his papers when the warehouse they were kept in at Sault Sainte Marie burned down. Fire was a common danger in the 1600s, when most buildings were made of wood.

A FINAL PARTING

☞ Marquette falls ill

☞ Explorers never meet again

At St. Francis Xavier mission at the end of the trip, Marquette was very ill. He had **dysentery**, a severe infection of the intestines caused by drinking dirty water. He rested at the mission and said goodbye to Jolliet. The two men never saw each other again. Less than two years later, Marquette died in the wilderness near Lake Michigan.

End of the Road

Jolliet and Marquette led a wave of French exploration. Neither man won much praise, but towns today bear their names and memorials honor their achievements.

Vanished!

In 1697, Jolliet became a professor of hydrography in Quebec. In 1700, he headed to his home on Anticosti Island. He never returned to Quebec. Historians assume that he died on Anticosti that same year.

MISSION IMPOSSIBLE

- Marquette preaches to the Illinois
- Dies in the wilderness

When he left the Illinois people in 1673, Marquette promised to return. Sick and weak, he managed to go back and preach to the Illinois on Easter Sunday in 1675. On his way back to St. Ignace, he was too ill to travel. He died (right) on May 18, 1675, aged just 37, near today's Ludington, Michigan. A river, lake, and other places in the area bear his name. Marquette's body was taken back to the mission at St. Ignace. The journal of his travels was published in Paris in 1681.

BACK IN BUSINESS

- Jolliet supports his family
- Sets up fisheries in the north

When the French government was reluctant to allow Jolliet to explore again, he returned to business. By 1679, he was married and had two children. He needed to take care of his family. He set up cod, whale, and seal **fisheries** at his Mingan (left) and Anticosti Island properties. After the English raided and burned his buildings in 1690, Jolliet rebuilt his businesses.

GO NORTH!

+ Jolliet sent on expedition

+ Meets the Inuit

In 1694, a merchant named François Viennay-Pachot employed Jolliet to explore the coast of Labrador. Jolliet and three sons sailed north with a group of 18 men. Jolliet drew a map of the coastline as they traveled. He also drew sketches (below right) and made detailed notes about the landscape and the people. Jolliet described meeting several Inuit, and buying seal meat and oil from them. He also made notes about their language, writing that he found it easy to understand. On his return, Jolliet sent a map of Labrador's coast to the French king, Louis XIV.

My Explorer Journal

★ **Imagine you are a news reporter who is writing about the death of Louis Jolliet. Using information in this book, write an obituary of the explorer summing up his main achievements.**

ANOTHER FRENCH EXPLORER

☛ **La Salle claims Louisiana**

☛ **Takes all the credit**

The French government gave little credit to Jolliet and Marquette for their exploration of the Mississippi. However, their expedition paved the way for other French explorers who followed. In 1682, René-Robert Cavelier, Sieur de La Salle, sailed down the Mississippi to the Gulf of Mexico. He claimed all the land for the French and named it Louisiana (left). The French settled Louisiana and used the Mississippi as a trade route—just as Louis Jolliet had suggested they should do.

GLOSSARY

calumet A long-stemmed pipe used by Native peoples as a sign of peace

canal An artificial waterway for vessels

capsized Overturned in the water

cartography The science of drawing maps

caulk To seal gaps between pieces of wood

colonize To settle an area and bring it under control of another country

compass A device that uses Earth's magnetic field to indicate the direction of north

convert To give up one religion for another, or to persuade someone else to do so

coureur de bois French for "runner of the woods," meaning a fur trapper

dialects Forms of a language spoken in specific areas

dysentery A serious infection of the intestines that causes severe diarrhea

extinct Having no living members

fisheries Areas where fish are caught on a commercial basis

hydrography The study and mapping of bodies of water such as lakes, rivers, and oceans

interpreters People who translate what people are saying into another language

investors People who fund a venture in the hopes of receiving more money in return

Jesuit A member of the Society of Jesus, a Roman Catholic order that does missionary work

mission The place where a missionary works

missionary Someone sent to promote Christianity in a foreign country

navigation Accurately determining one's location, planning and following a route

portage Carrying a boat on land between two areas on a river

profits Financial gain

pungent Describes something strong smelling

rapids A fast-flowing part of a river

sagamity Porridge made from corn and water

spiritual Related to religious belief

tributaries Rivers that flow into a larger river

wigwams Dome-shaped tents or huts

wilderness A wild, uninhabited, and inhospitable region

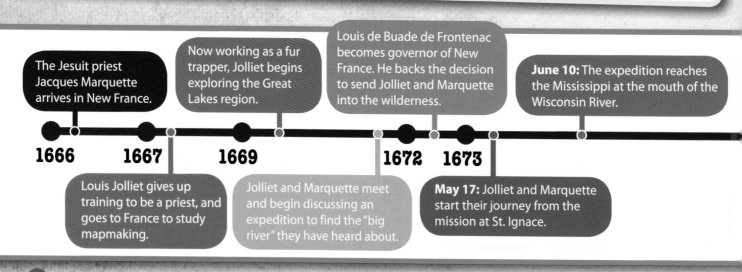

The Jesuit priest Jacques Marquette arrives in New France.

Now working as a fur trapper, Jolliet begins exploring the Great Lakes region.

Louis de Buade de Frontenac becomes governor of New France. He backs the decision to send Jolliet and Marquette into the wilderness.

June 10: The expedition reaches the Mississippi at the mouth of the Wisconsin River.

1666 **1667** **1669** **1672** **1673**

Louis Jolliet gives up training to be a priest, and goes to France to study mapmaking.

Jolliet and Marquette meet and begin discussing an expedition to find the "big river" they have heard about.

May 17: Jolliet and Marquette start their journey from the mission at St. Ignace.

ON THE WEB

www.historymuseum.ca/virtual-museum-of-new-france/the-explorers/louis-jolliet-1673-1694/
A biography of Jolliet from the Virtual Museum of New France. The site also has a biography of Jacques Marquette.

www.newadvent.org/cathen/09690a.htm
A biography of the missionary Father Marquette from the Catholic Encyclopedia.

www.encyclopediaofarkansas.net/encyclopedia/entry-detail.aspx?entryID=2208
A summary of the journey from the Encyclopedia of Arkansas History & Culture.

http://content.wisconsinhistory.org/cdm/ref/collection/tp/id/45904
A copy of Marquette's original hand-drawn map of the Mississippi River.

www.mrnussbaum.com/history-2-2/marquette/
A student-friendly site with details of Jolliet and Marquette's expedition on the Mississippi.

BOOKS

Harkins, Susan, and William Harkins. *Father Jacques Marquette* (Profiles in American History). Mitchell Lane Publishers, 2008.

Larkin, Tanya. *Jacques Marquette and Louis Jolliet: Explorers of the Mississippi*. Rosen Central, 2004.

Petrie, Kristin. *Marquette and Jolliet* (Explorers). Checkerboard Library, 2007.

Zelenyj, Alexander. *Marquette & Jolliet: Quest for the Mississippi* (In the Footsteps of Explorers). Crabtree Publishing Company, 2007.

July 17: The expedition turns back north near the mouth of the Arkansas River.

In Quebec, Louis Jolliet marries Claire-Françoise Bissot, daughter of a wealthy fur trader.

The French authorities give Louis Jolliet Anticosti Island as a reward for his achievements.

Now a professor of hydrography, Jolliet leaves Quebec for Anticosti Island. He never returns and is presumed to have died there.

1674   1675   1680   1682   1700

September: Marquette falls sick. Jolliet leaves him at Green Bay and continues the journey to Quebec.

May 17: Jaques Marquette dies in the wilderness after preaching to the Illinois people at Easter.

April 9: Having traveled down the Mississippi, René-Robert Cavelier, Sieur de La Salle claims the whole valley for France under the name Louisiana.

INDEX

J 910.0922 O'BRIEN

O'Brien, Cynthia.
Explore with
Marquette and Jolliet

R4003063829